Embrace Your Writer's Block

10 steps to breathe new life into your writing project

by Frank Ewert

work
with
words

franklin, tennessee

ISBN 978-8-9918016-0-7

Library of Congress Control Number: 2024925795

For bulk sale discounts, please send an email to jfe@workwithwords.co

Work with Words, LLC
Franklin, TN
615-624-0387

workwithwords.co

Cover design and interior layout by Caio Batista

Illustrations generated by Caio Batista, using Midjourney, an AI image generator

TABLE OF CONTENTS

This workbook is dedicated to every person who has ever wondered if they're a "real" writer.

(My answer is always a resounding "Yes!")

INTRODUCTION

When your writing project stalls or goes off the rails, it's tempting to just step away.

Sometimes, that's exactly what you need. Time to reflect and recharge. Space to see the forest and the trees.

However, this pause can easily turn into an indefinite hiatus. The longer you're away from your desk, the harder it is to return. Your project begins to taunt you. Every time you're brave enough to open your word processor, you're immediately frozen by overwhelm and slam your laptop shut. Your project stays stuck.

In case you can't tell, I'm writing from experience. I published my first book—a collection of short stories—when I was twenty-four. It wasn't a bestseller, but I was so proud. After years of daydreams, I'd finally written a real book.

But then life happened, and I stopped writing. Some of my reasons for stopping were reasonable: a move, a job change, a baby. Others were less obvious and more insidious. Latent anxieties slowly ate away at my confidence. Before I knew it, I went from being "on a break" to being unable to write.

The result? A decade of believing that I wasn't actually a writer after all. That writing was something I did once, just like that guy we all know who played football in high school.

However, that wasn't the end of my story. Not hardly.

Thanks to a series of encouraging voices, I rediscovered my passion for writing. I not only write for myself but also help others bring their books to life through coaching, ghostwriting, and editing. All because I learned how to embrace and write through my writer's block.

Like me, you've probably tried to "think your way through" this obstacle. Many good books have been written about creativity and finding your voice. Surely you just need to find the right one to set you free, right?

Sadly, no.

If you want to break through your writer's block, you need to wrestle with words on the page. By "words" I mean your words, and by "page" I mean something that you're actively writing. There's simply no other way to get back on track.

Getting unstuck takes time. If you're anything like me, you want to be in the clear already. You'll do anything you can to speed up this process and get back to your normal flow. I encourage you not to do that.

Instead, take your time. If you show up here day after day, you'll experience real growth and progress. By the end of the ten days, you'll have written over 7,500 words. Do that three times, and you'll be over 20,000. That's one-third of most books.

I believe you can do that. Are you ready to give yourself a chance?

HOW TO USE
THIS WORKBOOK

Like I said in the Introduction: if you want to break through your writer's block, you need to wrestle with your words. That's why I designed this workbook to be an interactive experience.

THE WORKBOOK'S DAILY RHYTHMS

Each day provides you with three things:

1. An encouraging reflection
2. A writing prompt
3. A set of blank lined pages

Throughout the workbook, each day builds upon the last. Some of the exercises are fun and will help you rediscover the joy of writing. Others will be a painful challenge. Don't skip either. Trust the process and give yourself to your words.

WRITE BY HAND

"Can't I type out my writing responses?" you might ask. "That'll be faster and more comfortable."

Here's the thing: you'll get a lot more out of this process if you complete the exercises by hand.

For starters, this workbook isn't a race. Going faster is not necessarily better. In fact, it might be counterproductive. There's much to be gained by moving slowly.

Second, this workbook will not remove every ounce of discomfort from your writing life. It's not supposed to. Instead, it'll teach you how to sit and write in the presence of discomfort, when appropriate.

Writing by hand helps on both fronts.

Our brains typically move faster than our pens. The sentence we thought we were writing meanders away from our expectations. Sometimes it feels like the words literally change as we're writing them. Why? Because we learn as we write. The sentence you end up writing is almost always more valuable than what you set out to say.

Also, it's tiring to write by hand, but you can do it! When you get to the end of your daily pages, you'll feel a physical sensation of accomplishment. A sensation that's very hard to come by when you're clickety-clacking your way through a Word document.

SET YOUR SCENE

That said, this experience shouldn't feel like a punishment. Indeed, I encourage you to mindfully create your experience so you can truly delight in this work.

Find your favorite writing tools and devote them to this task. For example, whenever I write by hand, I use Pentel EnerGel Liquid Gel Ink pens. No one's paying me to say that: I simply like the way their ink flows, allowing me to move my hand effortlessly across the page.

Also, choose where you're going to complete this writing. It doesn't matter if you do it at a quiet desk or in a noisy coffee shop. What matters is that the place you pick is a place where you feel free to be creative. I do a lot of my creative work at Starbucks. For whatever reason, my mind is wide open there, and my fingers fly in a way that doesn't come as naturally in my home office.

Of course, sometimes there are constraints. You might have to do these exercises during your subway commute or at the kitchen table in the evenings after your children have finally gone to bed. Even there, however, there is room for your creativity. Find something small that you can do to make those times and spaces your own.

CHOOSE YOUR RHYTHMS

As you've probably noticed, this workbook offers you 10 days of writing. That means you can complete this workbook in two weeks.

I do not recommend going any faster. Completing the workbook in one setting just won't give you the same value. It's beneficial to have time to breathe in between the exercises.

That said, you are free to take more time. Perhaps you want three days to complete an exercise. Perhaps longer. There's no right or wrong timeline. You get to decide what's right for you.

My only advice is that you set a timeline before you get started. Chart your journey on your calendar. Give yourself deadlines. If you don't meet them, that's okay. No one's going to fail you. However, you're far more likely to finish this workbook—and actually move your project forward—if you do a little planning upfront.

HAVE FUN AND PLAY AROUND

It's easy for us to take our writing too seriously. It's also paralyzing. How can we put words down on a first draft when we're demanding eloquent perfection of every sentence?

Here, I invite you—indeed, I implore you!—to give yourself permission to play. To be messy, even. Treat this workbook like a playground. It's a place for delight and imperfection. A safe place where you can wonder aloud.

Because there's no better way to rediscover the joy of writing and move your project forward.

Day 1

It's okay to be stuck

Embrace Your Writer's Block

"One's true strength rarely lies in the capacities and faculties of which one is proud, but frequently in those one regards as unimportant or even as weaknesses."

— W. H. Auden, "Introduction to Tales of Grimm and Andersen"

DAY 1: IT'S OKAY TO BE STUCK

As a writer, the realization that you're stuck can feel like a terminal diagnosis.

No one else can see that anything is amiss. At first, that's a relief. But then, as days drag on and writing continues to be a struggle, powerful fears set in. You start to worry that you'll never finish your project. You wonder if your writing talent has vanished.

Maybe it was never even real in the first place.

I know firsthand just how heavy these feelings are. I've felt them multiple times in my own writing career. I can only imagine how I would have responded if someone told me, "Hey, it's okay that you're stuck."

And yet, here I am, telling *you* that it's okay that you're stuck.

In fact, I'm going to go one step further and say that it is *good* that you're stuck.

Are you still with me?

Over the next ten days, you'll reflect on what makes you want to write, consider what it means to be stuck, and learn what you can do to keep going.

Am I promising that you'll break through to the other side with ease? No. I don't believe in magic formulas or cheat codes that allow you to bypass adversity. If that's what you're looking for, I'm sorry. You'll need to look elsewhere.

What I'm offering you is an opportunity to breathe and gain some perspective. I probably don't know you, so I can't speak directly into your situation. However, I've been a stuck writer, and I've also helped other stuck writers. These experiences have given me some pretty useful tools. I'm confident they'll benefit you and your writing.

What do you have to do? Simply write. This workbook comes with plenty of blank space, and I urge you to take advantage of it. The only way to get past your "stuckness" is to write your way through it.

If you're ready, let's get started.

DAY 1:
IT'S OKAY TO BE STUCK

PROMPT:

Reflect on your life right now. What things bring a smile to your face? Describe one (or more!) of these things. Write as if you were describing them to your childhood best friend.

Day 2

Recover your silly side

Embrace Your Writer's Block

"It was charming to see how these girls danced. They had no spectators but the apple-pickers on the ladders. They were very glad to please them, but they danced to please themselves . . . and you could no more help admiring, than they could help dancing. How they did dance!"

— Charles Dickens, The Battle of Life

DAY 2: RECOVER YOUR SILLY SIDE

I tend to take myself and my work seriously. This impulse comes from a well-meaning place. I love words and want to use them well. Also, I want to write about things that matter. I want to move my readers to think and do new things.

This workbook is no different. I'd love for this workbook to change your life. At the very least, I hope it encourages you to keep writing.

So, why on earth would I tell you to "recover your silly side"?

Simply because your ability to write hinges upon your ability to play. I'm not saying that you must be silly if you want to write. I just think that you'll never enjoy this work if you don't remember and rediscover the joy of pure play.

Kids often discover their passions by accident. We see a young girl playacting and are struck by her mimicry. "She's going to be on stage one day," we say. "Just you wait and see!"

Elsewhere, a boy is overheard singing as he pushes toy cars around the coffee table. "He can really carry a tune!" we gush. Soon he's in voice lessons, destined for a childhood of choir solos and music recitals.

Neither child set out to "be creative." They simply did things they enjoyed to make the hours pass by. Others who took note and encouraged them to hone their natural gifts.

Sometimes, well-meaning adults spoil the fun. Actually, well-meaning adults spoil the fun *most of the time.* We want talented kids to take their gifts seriously. That's why we thrust them into lessons and command them to conquer their stage fright.

Is there anything wrong with taking lessons or facing one's fears? Of course not. These steps may even be crucial elements of an artist's journey. However, we must recognize that these efforts can be real joy-killers. Your son or daughter can grow up to play the piano beautifully without having truly played for years.

And that's why, today, you're going to sit down and recover some of *your* childhood play.

DAY 2:
RECOVER YOUR SILLY SIDE

PROMPT:

What did you like to do when you were six years old? Specifically, what did you do just because you loved doing it, whether or not it caught someone's attention or earned you praise? Describe what that was, why you liked doing it, and how it made you feel.

*Thanks to Fraser Martens for coming up with this prompt and allowing me to use it here.

Day 3

You're stuck because your project matters

Embrace Your Writer's Block

" Resistance obstructs movement only from a lower sphere to a higher. It kicks in when we seek to pursue a calling in the arts, launch an innovative enterprise, or evolve to a higher station morally, ethically, or spiritually. "

— Steven Pressfield, The War of Art

DAY 3: YOU'RE STUCK BECAUSE YOUR PROJECT MATTERS

Back on Day 1, I declared, "It is good that you're stuck." However, I didn't explain myself. I deliberately left you to wonder what I could possibly mean. Today, let's return to that point and explore how being stuck can actually be a good thing.

Here's what I believe: being stuck is a sign that you're growing. The thing you're writing has pushed you into unfamiliar territory. As a result, your brain is tapping the brakes. It wisely recognizes you need to take this part slow to maximize your learning.

Does that eliminate your frustration? No. It most certainly does not. You probably feel a little like my youngest son. He watches his older sister and older brother very carefully, and he's very aware when they get to enjoy privileges that he doesn't. "Why does she get to stay up and watch TV?" he'll demand when I tell him it's his bedtime.

Well, I have good news for that writing child within you. Being stuck means that you're growing up. It means that your creativity is maturing.

Immature writers don't get stuck because they have undeveloped filters. Like young children, they wholeheartedly believe that everything they produce is glorious. And there's nothing wrong with that. Every child deserves praise and attention for their fledgling bursts of creativity. Without it, they wouldn't keep going.

Eventually, though, children need to learn some discernment. Partly because they need to realize that Dad can't preserve every single stick figure doodle. But more importantly, they need to discern what special things *they* have to offer the world. When they learn to do this, they begin to create what *only they* can create.

You, my friend, are experiencing this development.

What came easily before was good and not to be dismissed. You should be proud of it.

However, what's coming is better. That's what your writer's block is telling you. And that's why it is *good* that you're stuck.

DAY 3:
YOU'RE STUCK BECAUSE YOUR PROJECT MATTERS

PROMPT:

Use the following pages to do two things:

1. Describe your project as messily as you can. Don't pick your words too carefully.

2. Answer this question: "What questions do I need to ask in order to complete this project?" Don't worry about answering those questions right now. Just let yourself wonder and take note of your wonderings.

Day 4

Befriend your inner critic

Embrace Your Writer's Block

"All the things I choose to put in my head are what make me, me. I plan to choose wisely."

— Bob (in Bob by Wendy Mass & Rebecca Stead)

DAY 4: BEFRIEND YOUR INNER CRITIC

You're probably familiar with the concept of the "inner critic"—the voice in your head that provides color commentary on every thought you think and every move you make.

If you're anything like me, that voice constantly makes you cringe. It rarely has nice things to say. It's too busy pointing out your flaws and worrying about what other people think.

In other words, your inner critic can be a real jerk.

Our natural impulse is to drown out this voice. We metaphorically plug our ears while shouting, "Nah nah nah nah nah, I can't hear you!"

The trouble with this approach is that it gets in the way of our writing. Since the inner critic speaks in our head, its voice is awfully hard to ignore. And once it breaks through our fragile barriers, we typically stop writing. "I'll just wait until he's gone and try again later," we think.

You and I both know what happens "later."

My friend and fellow writer Jonathan Rogers suggests a different approach. "Your inner critic isn't an enemy," he says. Instead, it's simply "an overly talkative friend who sometimes needs to be told to be quiet."

Like it or not, our inner critic can say things that we need to hear. It can even help us refine our work. That's why Jonathan encourages writers to "befriend" their inner critic. Because, if we're honest, we rarely heed feedback from our enemies. We might listen to what a bully has to say, but we're only going to respond with seething anger. We don't learn anything.

A friend, on the other hand, is someone who will be quiet and listen when you ask them to. They love you, and if they sense that you're not getting anything from their words, they'll keep them to themselves. (Unlike enemies, who tend to just get louder.)

Which is all to say: if you want your inner critic to leave you alone for a while, you'd be wise to turn it into a pal.

DAY 4:
BEFRIEND YOUR INNER CRITIC

PROMPT:

This one is uncomfortable. However, it's important, so don't skip it. And more importantly, don't half-ass it.

What does your inner critic think about your current project? Write its thoughts in all their gory, honest detail. Is it cussing you out? Make sure those four-letter words show up on the page.

Don't worry about refuting or correcting your inner critic today. Just let it vent. (Believe it or not, you'll both feel better afterwards.)

When you're finished, put the pages aside and do something nice for yourself. Something truly delightful.

Day 5

Be derivative

Embrace Your
Writer's Block

"A wonderful flaw about human beings is that we're incapable of making perfect copies. Our failure to copy our heroes is where we discover where our own thing lives. That is how we evolve."

— Austin Kleon, Steal Like an Artist

DAY 5: BE DERIVATIVE

If there's one thing we writers dread, it's sounding like someone else. We want to show up as ourselves. We don't want to be considered a cheap knock-off.

This fear will sabotage your first draft quicker than you can say "Bob's your uncle." (I know that nobody says that anymore, but work with me, alright?) Once you start to worry that you sound like someone else, every sentence you write will ring out in that other person's voice.

Which is why I'm encouraging you, today, to be derivative.

If that makes you uncomfortable, think back to Day 2, when I encouraged you to reconnect with your silly side. How do kids learn how to do things? By copying others. It's how they learn to speak and eat with silverware and use colorful language and all sorts of other delightful actions.

You might think you're too old for that, but you're wrong. As Austin Kleon reminds us, the greatest artists steal like crazy. They don't pretend to be original. On the contrary, they celebrate their influences. "Look at this cool thing!" they cry. "Isn't it awesome that I get to do it too?"

Some, of course, take it too far. They deceive us—and sometimes themselves—into thinking that they came up with things all by their own bad selves. And they are being bad. To themselves, more than to anyone else.

When we openly imitate and interact with others, we inevitably add our own slant. Our unique experiences and perspectives bleed into the work. We make it our own and, in so doing, affect the thing we're imitating. We grow, and our readers get to grow too.

So, are you ready to embrace your inner copycat?

DAY 5:
BE DERIVATIVE

PROMPT:

First, pick a writer. Any writer. Doesn't have to be your favorite, but it should at least be someone you respect.

Next, reread your inner critic's comments from Day 4's exercise. All of them. Yes, every single word.

When you return to these pages, it's time for you to thoughtfully defend yourself. That's right, you're going to push back and argue with your inner critic. The only catch is that you need to do so in the voice/style of the writer you chose above.

Again, please don't half-ass this. Get into the spirit of things. That author is defending you with vehemence. With righteous anger, even. They're downright furious that anyone would dare to criticize you or your project.

What you write should feel exuberant and over the top. If it's not, erase and try again.

Day 6

Craft a simple plan that's full of holes

Embrace Your Writer's Block

"Creativity is about connections, and connections are not made by siloing everything off into its own space. New ideas are formed by interesting juxtapositions, and interesting juxtapositions happen when things are out of place."

— Austin Kleon, Keep Going

DAY 6: CRAFT A SIMPLE PLAN THAT'S FULL OF HOLES

For some people, the act of planning is a magical delight. They go about plotting vacations and scripting their lives with glee. When you need an event to be "just so," they're the people you call, because they'll deliver that and then some.

To others, "plan" is a four-letter word. The mere thought makes their throats constrict. They insist on being wild and free to do whatever they please, relishing the ability to be spontaneous and go with the flow.

I don't want to say that these approaches are wrong. That would be judgmental. (And besides, I hate either/or's and have never met a label I couldn't evade.)

But I do think that, when it comes to writing, both of these approaches are unhelpful.

Writers in the first camp have a tendency to get lost in their outline and world-building. "I'm going to get started on my story," they say, "but first I need to flesh things out."

Meanwhile, writers in the opposite camp—commonly called "pantsers"—can find it a struggle to stick with a project. Talk to them on Monday, and they'll excitedly tell you about their coming-of-age memoir. Tuesday, though, it turns out that they're writing a literary novel. By Thursday, they're hard at work on the script for a comedy TV pilot.

I'm going to go out on a limb and assume that you fall into one of these two camps. Don't take it personally. I just don't think you'd bother reading this book if that weren't true. And I only say that because I've spent time in both.

That's why I want you to craft a simple plan that's full of holes. It's wise to know where you're at (Point A) and where you want to go (Point Z). It's probably even a good idea to identify some stops along the way (Points B, C, and D). But once you've done that, it's time to stop planning and start writing.

Planners and pantsers alike will find this exercise uncomfortable.

That's okay. That's the point.

DAY 6:
CRAFT A SIMPLE PLAN
THAT'S FULL OF HOLES

PROMPT:

Capture the points I outlined in today's reflection: A, Z, B, C, and D. (Preferably in that order.)

Write no more than one paragraph—but at least two sentences—per point.

After that, write whatever comes to mind. It could be general notes. It could be a verbal sketch. It could be the first words of your next draft. It doesn't matter what it is or what you call it. What matters is that you write.

Day 7

Be unremarkable

Embrace Your Writer's Block

"It seems to me now that the plain state of being human is dramatic enough for anyone; you don't need to be a heroin addict or a performance poet to experience extremity. You just have to love someone."

— Katie Carr (in How to be Good by Nick Hornby)

DAY 7: BE UNREMARKABLE

I don't know about you, but I find that starting things is easy.

I feel pretty darn good on day one. I might even make it through the first week without too much trouble. But eventually, I bump into some resistance that prompts me to question my new endeavor.

The obstacle, whatever it is, always feels legit. "I would have put in the time," I tell myself, "but today just doesn't work. I'll definitely make it happen tomorrow."

Tomorrow, of course, comes with its own legit excuses. Soon, tomorrow after tomorrow turns into a search for a newer, better program that will actually work.

Starting may be easy. Repeatedly showing up is anything but.

Of course, you don't need me to tell you that. We both know this hard truth. Yet, we also convince ourselves time and time again this *[insert new thing here]* will be different. That our mindset is finally where it needs to be. That whatever life hack we've been sold is going to be a gamechanger. Yadda yadda yadda.

This is the part where I'm supposed to offer the secret key to perseverance. The lesson that eliminated every temptation "from my path

But I don't have anything like that. I still face plenty of temptations. There are still days—more than I care to admit—that I have to force myself to sit still and put words down on the page.

What helps me is this reminder: I don't need to produce remarkable stuff every day. I just need to show up and write some more. And then do the same thing again the next day.

Some days the magic is palpable. I get into a groove, the words flow, and I'm ecstatic. Other days, I'm decidedly uninspired by the results. Thankfully, I'm not out to impress myself. Or others, for that matter. My job is simply to write, and just doing that is enough.

DAY 7:
BE UNREMARKABLE

PROMPT:

Building on Day 6's outline, fill the following pages with round two of freewriting.

An important note: if you've already written material for your project, you may not reuse it here. What you write in these pages should be new. It's okay if it echoes what you've written elsewhere. I simply don't want you to copy and paste.

You're doing this work for your own sake, so don't sell yourself short or deprive yourself.

Day 8

Stop editing

Embrace Your Writer's Block

"Every first draft is a dumpster fire. All writing begins by being awful and only starts to shine through rewrites, beta reading, and editing. A draft is still a baby; it's unfair to judge it by the standards of a grown-up book."

— Rob Fitzpatrick, Write Useful Books

DAY 8: STOP EDITING

Once you're in the thick of your project, it's natural to heighten your expectations.

It's tempting, at this stage, to start being picky. You sit down to write, bang out a few sentences, and then pause to consider what you've written. "Hmmm," you think, "that's not as good as yesterday's batch." So you hit the backspace button a few times—until you've got a fresh, clean screen to work with again—and you start over.

This isn't always a mistake. Sometimes you realize in the midst of writing that the point you're trying to make has shifted. The words you started with no longer support the path you're on.

However, you must never dismiss these no-longer-necessary words out of hand. Your future readers may not need them, but you certainly did. Without them, you wouldn't be headed in the direction you are now.

There's an old saying in one of E. M. Forster's books: "How can I tell what I think till I see what I say?" I learned it in my first creative writing class, and I think it's a wise comment. When we're cautious with our words, we're actually being cautious with our thoughts. What effect do you think that has on your work?

Don't misunderstand me: I am not suggesting you should always avoid editing. Many a book would have been far stronger if its author and publishers had pruned more carefully.

Just keep in mind that your final product will probably bear little—if any—resemblance to your first draft. That's not a failure. On the contrary, that's a success. It means that you learned something while you were writing. Why would you give up that chance to grow?

DAY 8:
STOP EDITING

PROMPT:

Reflect on your past writing successes. (Don't you dare say that you have none.) What surprised you as you wrote them?

It's possible that you won't be able to think of anything, and that's okay. Consider this your invitation to be on the lookout for such gifts as you go forward. In fact, start looking for those lessons by moving on with your next round of writing.

Challenge yourself not to erase, cross out, or otherwise edit your words as you write. See what happens.

Day 9

Find teammates

Embrace Your Writer's Block

"When people ask me what I think is the single most important factor in an artist's sustained productivity, I know I am supposed to say something like "solitude," or "an independent income," or "childcare." All of these things are good and many people have said so, but what I think is better and more important than any of these things is what I call "a believing mirror."

Put simply, a believing mirror is a friend to your creativity—someone who believes in you and your creativity."

— Julia Cameron, The Artist's Way

DAY 9: FIND TEAMMATES

Writing is a team sport.

That statement might sound counterintuitive. Anyone who's written anything can fairly protest that writing is a solo act. You sit in a solitary chair, stare at a solitary screen, and type on a solitary keyboard. This technology may be specific to our time and place, but that sentence wouldn't change a whole lot if you took it back two hundred years.

And yet, we writers never arrive at our words on our own. We often begin writing because others have stopped and marveled at our words. How else would we ascertain our gift?

So, what kind of teammates do you want?

I suggest that, when you're looking for teammates, you want to find people who address at least one of two needs: encouragement and challenge.

As I've already noted, very few people know intuitively that they are gifted writers. We need encouragement to keep on going. People who say, "I read what you wrote, and I connected with it. Keep going! I want to read more!"

Yet, we also need readers who are willing and able to interrogate us. "What did you mean by [this]?" or "I didn't understand [that]. Tell me more." Their curiosity sparks ours. Without that ignition, we wouldn't advance nearly as far.

That said, both needs can be insufficiently addressed. Some readers too readily affirm our work. Which is to say that they mindlessly affirm our work. Do not mistake a social media "like" as heartfelt encouragement.

Likewise, some people provide antagonistic opposition. They critique our writing, but their feedback is anything but constructive. Under the guise of "edits," they tear us down and undermine our work. They're too busy trying to find all our errors to actually love and encourage us.

How do you tell the difference? Simply by answering this question: "What people make me want to write?"

Surround yourself with such people, and all will be well.

DAY 9:
FIND TEAMMATES

PROMPT:

Describe the people in your life who lovingly
support and/or challenge your work.

Is anyone supporting and/or challenging you
without love? If so, what would it take to
replace them with better voices?

Day 10

Trust yourself

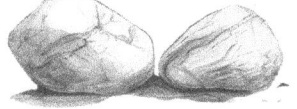

Embrace Your
Writer's Block

"Ultimately you write alone. And ultimately you and you alone can judge your work. The judgment that a work is complete—this is what I meant to do, and I stand by it—can come only from the writer, and it can be made rightly only by a writer who's learned to read her own work."

— Ursula K. Le Guin, Steering the Craft

DAY 10: TRUST YOURSELF

As much as we writers want affirmation—a want that is very healthy—we must be careful not to mistakenly seek validation in its place.

When we seek affirmation, we're asking our readers, "Can you see what I see when you look at the world?" When we seek validation, we're asking our readers, "What *should* I see when I look at the world?"

The difference is subtle, but it's a crucial subtlety.

Think of it another way: affirmations assure us that we've been seen and heard.

That's why it is essential for us writers to trust ourselves.

There's nothing wrong with requesting and accepting feedback. That's a good and wise move. But how do we discern which feedback is helpful and which feedback is not? That discernment must always come from within.

My encouragement here is simple: trust that you know best how to use your voice and what you have to say with it.

If you want to write and put your words out into the world, you must cultivate this kind of confidence. It's the only way for you to develop and own your unique voice, which is precisely the voice the world wants to hear.

DAY 10:
TRUST YOURSELF

PROMPT:

Reflect on your project, using the following questions as a guide:

1. To whom are you writing?
2. What do you want to tell them?
3. Why?

Answer as specifically as you can. The more clearly you know what you're up to, the more clearly you'll be able to write.

What's next?

Embrace Your
Writer's Block

"Getting what you want often scares you more than not getting it. As a young grad student, I worried like hell that I looked like a bimbo; now that I'm an old-maid schoolteacher, I worry that I don't. My point being, almost every time I was super-afraid, it was of the wrong thing."

— Mary Karr, Now Go Out There

Congratulations: you just finished two solid weeks of writing!

Before you re-assess the state of your project, I want to offer a final encouragement—one I'm borrowing from Julia Cameron.

In *The Artist's Way*, Cameron warns against the "How am I doing?" syndrome, noting the innocuous toxicity behind this question:

> This question is not "Is the work going well?"
> This question is "How does it look to them?"

Your final day of writing was an encouragement to trust yourself. That's probably the most important lesson in this exercise. It's also the hardest to stick with.

From here, your next step is pretty simple: keep showing up and keep writing. Don't be afraid of feedback, but don't judge yourself by what others think or say. They're not you. They don't see what you see. They don't have your voice.

Deep down, you know what "work going well" looks like for you. You know that it doesn't always feel awesome. You know when you need to buck up and just get it done. You also know when you need a friend to tell you that everything's okay.

Just keep showing up. Keep writing. Stay curious about yourself and your work, trusting that your curiosity will lead you right where you need to go.

ACKNOWLEDGEMENTS & RESOURCES

As I write this section, my wife is making turkey chili in her parents' kitchen. It's the day after Thanksgiving, and she's turning yesterday's leftovers into a new meal. This chili will feed the family hordes descending later and clear out the fridge, a true win-win.

In many ways, this book is a lot like that pot of chili. Every sentence here is my own, and yet I'm also riffing on the work of others.

For starters, I've heartily embraced the spirit of Austin Kleon's three books on creativity: *Steal Like an Artist*, *Show Your Work*, and *Keep Going*. You'd do well to read each one. If you've already read them, read them again.

I also owe a great debt to Julia Cameron and *The Artist's Way*. That classic helped me recover my ability to write. I embraced her "get writing" philosophy as I crafted this workbook, firmly agreeing that you can't read your way past writer's block.

Jonathan Rogers, who leads a writing community called The Habit (www.thehabit.co), has been another prominent influence in my writing. His workshops helped me knock off the rust after years of writer's block, and his weekly newsletter is a regular source of encouragement and hope.

Big thanks to all my beta readers, whose feedback sharpened and enhanced this workbook: Andrew Carter, Olivia d'Silva, Stuart Eglin, Marie Fuzzell, Lindsey Gallant, Joanna Gray, Fraser Martens, Claudia Mischke, and Andrew Nemr.

A special shout-out to Matthew Kimberley, who not only read the workbook but also gave me the idea (and the nudge) to create it in the first place.

Finally, this workbook would not exist without the collaboration and creativity of Caio Batista. After hearing my vision and reading my first draft, he presented me with the striking image of a rock cairn blocking a road (inspired by Carlos Drummond de Andrade's poem, "In the Middle of the Road."). That imagery elevated my work, as has every discussion we've had through the design process. I'm indebted to him for his consistent reminders to consider our reader-writers' tangible experience as they write through these ten days.

OTHER HELPFUL BOOKS

Art & Fear by David Bayles & Ted Orland

The Art of Memoir by Mary Karr

Bird by Bird by Anne Lamott

How to Begin by Michael Bungay Stanier

Steering the Craft by Ursula K. Le Guin

The War of Art by Steven Pressfield

Write Useful Books by Rob Fitzpatrick

Just don't let yourself be too busy reading to stick with your writing!

ABOUT THE AUTHOR

Frank Ewert is a writer who loves to edit. Or perhaps an editor who loves to write? (He's never sure which comes first.)

He's the author of *Embrace Your Writer's Block,* a workbook for writers who want to get their projects unstuck. He's also the author of *Blue Ice and Other Stories from the Rink,* a collection of short stories about ice hockey.

In 2021 he founded Work with Words. Under this umbrella, he publishes resources for writers and provides editing services. Learn more by visiting him online at workwithwords.co

Born and raised in the Fraser Valley of beautiful British Columbia, he now lives in Franklin, Tennessee, with his wife and kids.

www.ingramcontent.com/pod-product-compliance
Lightning Source LLC
Chambersburg PA
CBHW041538120626

46551CB00019B/2752